THOR & LOKI

IN THE LAND OF GIANTS

A
NORSE
MYTH

STORY BY
JEFF LIMKE

PENCILS AND INKS BY
RON RANDALL

SCANDINAVIA
Lands of the Norse

THOR & LOKI
IN THE LAND OF GIANTS

RUSSIA

FINLAND

SWEDEN

A
NORSE
MYTH

BALTIC
SEA

Lerner

LERNER BOOKS LONDON • NEW YORK • MINNEAPOLIS

THEIR ADVENTURES HAVE BEEN PASSED DOWN THROUGH THE MEDIEVAL WORK THE *PROSE EDDA*. THIS WORK WAS WRITTEN AROUND 1200 BY SNORRI STURLUSON, A POET AND POLITICIAN LIVING IN ICELAND. FOR THIS BOOK, AUTHOR JEFF LIMKE CONSULTED MODERN RETELLINGS OF THOR AND LOKI'S LEGENDARY JOURNEY TO THE LAND OF THE GIANTS, INCLUDING *BULFINCH'S MYTHOLOGY*, THE CLASSIC WORK OF AMERICAN THOMAS BULFINCH. ARTIST RON RANDALL CONSULTED NUMEROUS REFERENCE BOOKS ON MEDIEVAL VIKINGS AS WELL AS ART FROM THE ANCIENT NORSE PERIOD TO BRING TO LIFE THE VIVID IMAGES OF THIS STORY.

STORY BY JEFF LIMKE

PENCILS AND INKS BY RON RANDALL

COLOURING BY HI-FI DESIGN

LETTERING BY BILL HAUSER

First published in the United Kingdom in 2011 by
Lerner Books,
Dalton House,
60 Windsor Avenue,
London SW19 2RR

Website address: www.lernerbooks.co.uk

British Library Cataloguing in Publication Data

Limke, Jeff.
   Thor & Loki : in the land of giants. — (Graphic myths and legends)
   1. Thor (Norse deity) — Comic books, strips, etc. — Juvenile fiction. 2. Loki (Norse deity) — Comic books, strips, etc. — Juvenile fiction. 3. Children's stories — Comic books, strips, etc.
   I. Title II. Series
   741.5-dc22

   ISBN-13: 978 0 7613 6869 4

Printed in China
First published in the United States of America in 2010

TABLE OF CONTENTS

LOKI, MY BROTHER, YOU REALLY DON'T UNDERSTAND.

IN NORSE MYTHOLOGY, TWO GODS ARE VERY POPULAR.

ULTIMATELY, YOU NEED *STRENGTH* BECAUSE IT WILL ALWAYS GET YOU OUT OF WHATEVER TROUBLE YOU ARE IN.

THOR, THE GOD OF THUNDER, WAS STRONG AND CARRIED WITH HIM A MAGIC HAMMER CALLED *MJOLNIR*.

LOKI WAS KNOWN AS THE *TRICKSTER GOD* BECAUSE HE WOULD ALWAYS TRY TO FIND A CUNNING SOLUTION TO A PROBLEM AND—

NO, THOR, IT DOESN'T *ALWAYS* WORK THAT WAY.

A VISIT FROM THE GODS

HE SOMETIMES USED TRICKS TO OUTWIT BOTH ENEMIES AND FRIENDS.

LOOK, WE HAVE LEFT OUR HOME IN *ASGARD* TO JOURNEY TO *THE LAND OF GIANTS*.

THERE YOU'LL SEE THAT I'M RIGHT. BRAINS WILL ALWAYS BEAT BRAWN.

I DON'T KNOW WHY WE'RE DOING THIS. YOU KNOW I'M RIGHT.

I **DON'T** KNOW THAT.

YOU'RE JUST TRYING TO TRICK ME INTO SAYING YOU'RE RIGHT. YOU'RE ALWAYS TRYING TO DO THAT TO ME.

WELL, NO MORE. THIS TIME I'M GOING TO **PROVE** I'M RIGHT AND YOU'LL HAVE TO SAY YOU'RE WRONG.

MAYBE. ONLY TIME WILL TELL.

AND SPEAKING OF TIME, IT'S GETTING LATE AND WE WILL NEED A PLACE TO STAY.

LET'S ASK THIS FARMER TO LET US STAY WITH HIM AND HIS FAMILY TONIGHT. NO MORTAL WOULD TELL A GOD NO. THEY FEAR OUR STRENGTH TOO MUCH TO BE THAT FOOLISH.

YOU REALLY BELIEVE THAT STRENGTH IS ALWAYS THE KEY, DON'T YOU?

OF COURSE!

HELLOOOO!

WHAT'S GOING ON OUT HERE?!

I OUGHT TO—

—REALLY—

※

GOOD FARMER, WE NEED A PLACE TO STAY TONIGHT.

WE WERE HOPING YOU WOULD HAVE ROOM FOR US.

Y-YES, OF COURSE. I-I'M NOT SURE ABOUT SUPPER.

W-WE HAVE BARELY ENOUGH FOOD TO FEED MYSELF AND MY TWO CHILDREN.

NOT TO WORRY. WE GODS CAN HANDLE THAT. RIGHT, LOKI?

OF COURSE, THOR.

LET ME GET EVERYTHING READY FOR TONIGHT THEN.

HOW DO YOU LIKE MY GOATS, FARMER?

VERY TASTY.

BUT, LORD THOR, HOW WILL YOU TRAVEL TOMORROW IF YOU'VE BUTCHERED YOUR GOATS?

SHHHH, THJALFI.

IT'S QUITE ALL RIGHT, RASKOVA, YOUR BROTHER ASKS A GOOD QUESTION.

DON'T WORRY, BOY, YOU JUST EAT UP.

YOUR FATHER HAS BEEN KIND ENOUGH TO LET US SLEEP IN YOUR WARM HOUSE.

TOMORROW, I'LL TAKE CARE OF HOW THE CHARIOT GETS PULLED.

HE'S STRONG ENOUGH TO PULL IT HIMSELF IF HE HAS TO.

IF I HAVE TO.

JUST BE SURE TO THROW ALL YOUR BONES ONTO THE SKINS WHEN YOU'RE FINISHED.

AND DON'T BREAK ANY.

THE NEXT MORNING...

WHAT A GLORIOUS MORNING. WE SHOULD BE ABLE TO COMPLETE OUR JOURNEY TODAY WITH A GOOD RUN FROM MY—

GOAT?

WHO DISOBEYED MY RULE!

WHO BROKE TANNGRISNIR'S LEG?

I DID. I JUST CRACKED IT A BIT TO GET TO THE MARROW AND—

10

DIDN'T YOU LISTEN TO ME?

WHY SHOULDN'T I STRIKE YOU DEAD WHERE YOU STAND?

NO! STRIKE ME INSTEAD!

HE IS JUST A BOY. SURELY YOU DID FOOLISH THINGS WHEN YOU WERE A CHILD?

I'LL SAY.

YOU STAY OUT OF THIS!

JUST POINTING OUT THE MAN HAS A POINT, BROTHER.

PLEASE, LORD THOR, I BEG OF YOU. TAKE THE BOY AND THE GIRL WITH YOU.

THJALFI CAN SAIL OUR LITTLE FISHING BOAT AS WELL AS ANY MAN AND HE RUNS AS FAST AS THE WIND. HE CAN HELP PILOT YOU TO THE LAND OF GIANTS.

RASKOVA CAN COOK LIKE NO ONE ELSE AROUND HERE. SHE CAN KEEP YOU FAT AND CONTENT ON YOUR TRIP.

WELL, BROTHER, WHAT DO YOU SAY?

I'M THINKING, I'M THINKING.

VERY WELL. I ACCEPT YOUR DEAL.

THE CHILDREN SHALL ACCOMPANY US ON OUR TRIP.

WITH YOU I LEAVE TANNGRISNIR AND TANNGNJOSTR, WHO ARE AS CLOSE TO ME AS YOUR CHILDREN ARE TO YOU.

I TRUST NO FURTHER HARM WILL COME TO THEM. LIKEWISE, YOU CAN KNOW YOUR CHILDREN ARE SAFE WITH US GODS.

FATHER?

YOU ARE IN SAFE HANDS, LITTLE ONE. I WILL BE HERE WHEN YOU RETURN.

DID YOU SEE HOW THEY FEARED MY STRENGTH, LOKI?

YES, YOU HAD THEM TERRIFIED, THAT'S FOR SURE.

OF COURSE, I DID. THAT FARMER WAS SURE I WOULD DESTROY EVERYTHING HE HAD.

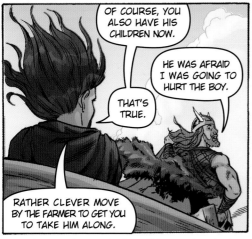

OF COURSE, YOU ALSO HAVE HIS CHILDREN NOW.

HE WAS AFRAID I WAS GOING TO HURT THE BOY.

THAT'S TRUE.

RATHER CLEVER MOVE BY THE FARMER TO GET YOU TO TAKE HIM ALONG.

HMM, YES, IT WAS.

AND THE GOATS.

HE'LL TAKE GOOD CARE OF THEM BECAUSE HE KNOWS WHAT I CAN DO IF HE DOESN'T.

OH YES, I'M SURE OF THAT TOO.

SO IT WOULD SEEM HE MANAGED TO KEEP HIS FAMILY ALIVE AND HIMSELF WELL FED NOW THAT HIS DAUGHTER CAN NO LONGER COOK FOR HIM.

IT'S A GOOD THING HE WAS SO SCARED OF YOUR *MUSCLES*, OR YOU'D HAVE NEVER PROMISED TO KEEP HIS FAMILY SAFE EVEN THOUGH ONE OF THEM DISOBEYED YOU.

YOU ... YOU ... JUST BE QUIET.

WE'RE HERE.

INTO THE LAND OF GIANTS

WELCOME TO THE LAND OF GIANTS.

I'M NOT SLOW. YOU JUST THINK IT'S SO WONDERFUL THAT YOU CAN RUN FAST AND I CAN'T.

JEALOUS YOU'RE JUST JEALOUS THAT'S ALL IT IS.

AHEM!

JEALOUS! OF WHAT? I CAN RUN FAST ENOUGH. JUST BECAUSE I CAN'T—

AND STOP TALKING SO FAST. YOU SOUND STUPID!

AHEM!

WHAT?

HE SAID, "AHEM!" THAT MEANS HE WANTS TO TALK, NOT YOU.

ABOUT WHAT?

ABOUT WHERE TO SLEEP TONIGHT? REMEMBER?

YOU DON'T HAVE TO YELL, YOU KNOW. WE'RE JUST KIDS.

YOU'RE JUST BEING NASTY.

NASTY? I'M THOR. *I'M THE LORD OF STORMS, THE THUNDERER.*

I'M A GOD.

WELL, THAT DOESN'T GIVE YOU THE RIGHT TO BE NASTY, TOO...

WHATEVER.

THERE'S A CAVE UP AHEAD A BIT, THAT'S BIG ENOUGH FOR ALL OF US TO STAY WARM.

I HAD IT UNDER CONTROL, BUT YOU HAD TO GO AND THROW YOUR LITTLE TANTRUM AND—

DON'T YOU START TOO.

START WHAT?

HERE IT IS.

SO WHAT DO YOU THINK?

I THINK YOU'RE GOING TO HAVE TO GET ME SOMETHING I CAN COOK.

THINK THAT WILL BE ENOUGH?

PROBABLY NEED A BIT MORE SINCE IT'S NOT JUST US AND FATHER.

LORD THOR, IF YOU WOULD BE SO KIND AS TO START THE FIRE.

GLADLY.

NOW GIVE ME A BIT OF TIME, AND WE'LL EAT AS WELL AS WHEN YOU FED US YOUR GOATS, LORD THOR.

LET'S MOVE DEEPER INTO THIS CAVE. IT'LL BE QUIETER AND SAFER WITHIN.

AND WHILE WE'RE IN THERE, I'LL CREATE A STORM OUTSIDE TO DRIVE THE ANIMAL AWAY.

WHAT DO YOU THINK IT IS, LORD LOKI? I'VE NEVER HEARD ANYTHING LIKE THAT.

IN ALL MY YEARS, I HAVEN'T EITHER.

NOT IN ASGARD, THAT'S FOR SURE.

I COMMAND A STORM!

NOW TO CATCH UP WITH THE OTHERS.

THAT STORM SHOULD KEEP US SAFE AND THE BEAST AT A DISTANCE.

IN ODIN'S NAME, WHAT IS THIS PLACE?

ISN'T IT GRAND? IT'S LIKE A PALACE!

WELL, I WOULDN'T SAY *THAT*, BUT IT'S STILL RATHER—

IMPRESSIVE.

SKRYMIR

WHERE ARE YOU TRAVELLING TO?

BEWARE GIANT, MY NAME IS THOR AND ALL HERE ARE UNDER MY PROTECTION.

HO, NO NEED TO BE AFRAID.

MY NAME'S SKRYMIR, AND I'M TRAVELLING TO THE HALL OF UTGARD-LOKI, KING OF THE GIANTS.

THE KING OF THE GIANTS. THAT'S WHERE WE'RE GOING.

SHHHHHH!

WELL, LET'S TRAVEL TOGETHER, THEN.

WELL, I'M NOT SO SURE.

YOU COULD JUST BE TAKING US SOMEWHERE TO EAT US.

NOT ENOUGH MEAT ON YOUR BONES TO MAKE A GIANT HAPPY.

LET ME CARRY YOU AND YOUR THINGS.

I CAN WALK FINE, BUT IF YOU'LL TAKE THIS WEIGHT OFF ME, YOU'LL GAIN A BIT OF MY TRUST.

LET'S GET WALKING THEN BECAUSE WE'RE JUST OVER A DAY'S JOURNEY AWAY.

SKRYMIR SAID WE COULD EAT FROM HIS BAG, BUT I CAN'T UNTIE THE LACES.

LATER THAT EVENING, AFTER SKRYMIR GOES TO SLEEP, THOR AND LOKI DECIDE TO *SCROUNGE* FOR SOME FOOD.

LET ME TRY.

IT'S ALL A TRICK. HE WOULD HAVE US STARVE.

BUT THOR IS NO GIANT'S FOOL!

I WILL SHOW HIM WHO IS THE FOOL!

26

27

THE HOME OF THE FROST GIANTS

NOW, BE VERY CAREFUL INSIDE. WATCH WHAT YOU SAY.

UTGARD-LOKI AND THE OTHER GIANTS WILL NOT TAKE KINDLY TO LITTLE ONES LIKE YOU BEING BOASTFUL.

WHO IS HE TO TELL ME NOT TO SPEAK OF MY GRAND DEEDS?

HE'S THE GIANT YOU COULD **BARELY WAKE**, REMEMBER?

VERY FUNNY, VERY FUNNY.

YOU WERE THE ONE WHO ARGUED YOUR STRENGTH COULD HANDLE ANYTHING.

IT WASN'T HOW CLEVER SOMEONE WAS. IT WAS HOW **STRONG**.

I STILL THINK THAT. LOOK AROUND, YOU THINK THESE GIANTS ARE GOING TO RESPECT SOME TRICK YOU PULL ON THEM?

OH, I THINK THEY WOULD RESPECT IT.

I DON'T, AND I'LL END UP HAVING TO PROVE YOU WRONG—

AGAIN.

I'M AFRAID THIS IS AS FAR AS YOU CAN GO.

NO ONE IS ALLOWED INSIDE UNLESS THEY CAN PROVE THEIR STRENGTH.

WHAT DID I SAY?

WAIT!

KREEEEEEEEEEEK

THUD!

HOW WAS *THAT*, BROTHER?

IT'S A START.

THE CHALLENGE OF THE GIANTS

YOU ARE UTGARD-LOKI, AND I AM THOR, GOD OF THUNDER.

BRING ON YOUR CHALLENGES.

YOU MUST EXCUSE MY IMPETUOUS BROTHER.

HE MEANS NO DISRESPECT.

HE IS VERY DIRECT IN HIS WAYS.

A BIT, SHALL WE SAY, UNSOPHISTICATED.

WE ARE MERE TRAVELLERS PASSING THROUGH.

YOUR KINSMAN SKRYMIR OFFERED US AN OPPORTUNITY TO VISIT YOUR FAMOUS HOLD AND WE ACCEPTED.

SO WE'LL JUST BE ON OUR WAY.

NO NEED TO SHOW US THE WAY. WE CAN SEE IT THROUGH YOUR—

STOP!!

THOR HAS ACCEPTED THE CHALLENGE OF THE GIANTS.

OUR LAWS SAY IF ONE TRAVELLER ACCEPTS THE CHALLENGE, THEN ALL ACCEPT.

WHICH OF YOU CHOOSES TO GO FIRST?

I THINK IT ONLY FAIR, SINCE MY BROTHER GOT US INTO YOUR LITTLE SET OF CONTESTS, THAT HE GO FIRST.

YOU SAID THAT IF ONE WERE IN, ALL WERE IN. THAT MEANS WE ALL MUST DO A CHALLENGE?

YES, EXCEPT FOR THE GIRL, YOU MUST ALL DO AT LEAST ONE.

VERY GOOD. THEN I THINK—

WHAT?? HOW COME I CAN'T?

PLEASE, RASKOVA. IT'S THEIR CONTEST, SO IT'S THEIR RULES.

LET'S NOT MAKE THEM ANGRY, OK?

THEN THE BOY SHALL GO FIRST AND SHOW YOU HOW THE LEAST OF US IS BETTER THAN YOU EXPECT.

SEEMS A BIT SMALL, EVEN FOR A NON-GIANT.

WHAT'S HE DO?

HE RUNS FASTER THAN ANYONE YOU HAVE EVER SEEN.

VERY WELL. I THINK WE HAVE HIS OPPONENT.

HUGI!

YOU SHALL RACE THREE TIMES.

EACH RACE'S WINNER IS DECIDED BY WHO RUNS THROUGH THAT DOORWAY FIRST.

YOUR SECOND RACE WILL BE BACK TO HERE, AND THE LAST WILL BE TO THE DOORWAY AGAIN.

ON YOUR MARKS.

GET SET.

GO!

NOT VERY IMPRESSIVE, THOR.

BUT THERE ARE MORE CHALLENGES. WHO DO YOU CHOOSE FOR THE SECOND CHALLENGE?

MY BROTHER, LOKI, OF COURSE.

E SEEMS A BIT NIMPRESSIVE.

HE IS A GOD. THE BOY WAS A HUMAN.

TO BEAT A HUMAN CHILD IS NOT A GREAT FEAT BY ANY MEASURE.

VERY WELL.

WHAT CAN YOUR BROTHER DO?

HE CAN EAT.

EAT??

EAT.

VERY GOOD!

A GIANT LOVES EATING ALMOST AS MUCH AS FIGHTING!

LOGI AWAITS YOU LOKI.

35

LOGI WINS!

THIS IS NOT HAPPENING.

YOU BOTH HAVE EMBARRASSED ME.

I WILL DO THE REST OF THESE CHALLENGES.

UTGARD-LOKI, JUST TELL ME WHAT THEY ARE, AND I WILL DO THEM.

VERY WELL.

I SHOW YOU THE NEXT TWO, BECAUSE SURELY YOU CAN BEAT AT LEAST ONE OF THEM.

DRINK THE HORN UNTIL IT'S DRY.

IF YOU FAIL TO DO THAT, THEN MERELY LIFT THE SLEEPING CAT.

THERE IS NO ONE ALIVE WHO CAN OUTDRINK ME!

JUST A MOMENT. I HAVE BARELY WHET MY THIRST.

AHHH, IT IS SO REFRESHING.

THUMP!

IF I DRINK ANYMORE, I WILL BURST.

I CAN'T GO ON.

THE CAT AWAITS.

JUST LIFT IT HIGH ENOUGH SO THAT ITS PAWS AND CLAWS DO NOT TOUCH THE FLOOR.

THIS SHOULD BE SIMPLE ENOUGH.

I WOULD BE WORRIED IF THIS WERE SOMETHING LARGER, LIKE A BULL, BUT NOT A HOUSE CAT, EVEN IF IT'S A GIANT'S HOUSE CAT.

UUUPPP!

ARRRRRHHH!!

AARRRRRHHHHH!!

AAAHHHHHHHHHHH!!

UUHHFFDDAAHH!

I'M AFRAID YOU FAILED THIS CHALLENGE TOO.

ALL RIGHT. BRING ON THIS LAST CHALLENGE.

IT CAN'T BE AS DIFFICULT AS THESE LAST TWO.

YOU CAN'T BE SERIOUS?

THIS IS THE LAST CHALLENGE?

OH, I'M VERY SERIOUS.

IF YOU COULDN'T FINISH ONE OF OUR HORNS NOR LIFT ONE OF OUR LITTLE PETS—

WHAT MAKES YOU THINK YOU CAN OUTWRESTLE THIS OLD CRONE?

IT'S ALL ABOUT STRENGTH, REMEMBER WHAT YOU TOLD ME.

I WARN YOU, OLD WOMAN, I DO NOT NORMALLY TREAT WOMEN THIS WAY—

BUT I WILL PIN YOU TO THE FLOOR.

WHUMP!

THOR-DUD-DUD-!

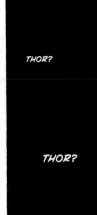

THOR?

THOR?

THOR?

ARE YOU ALL RIGHT?

I'M SORRY, BUT THE CRONE HAS BEATEN YOU.

I UNDERSTAND.

WE'LL LEAVE NOW.

THE **TRUTH**

BEFORE YOU GO, THERE IS SOMETHING YOU MUST KNOW.

WE HAVE NOT BEEN TRUTHFUL WITH YOU.

WE SAW YOU SAIL TOWARDS OUR LAND AND KNEW OF YOUR STRENGTH AND ANGER.

SO I MET YOU AT THE SHORE AS SKRYMIR TO TEST WHAT WE KNEW.

WHEN YOU STRUCK AT ME, YOU REALLY HIT THE GROUND, CREATING VALLEYS DEEPER THAN I AM TALL.

I SAW THEN HOW POWERFUL YOU WERE AND KNEW WE GIANTS WERE NO MATCH FOR YOU. SO WE DEVISED A TRICK TO SEND YOU AWAY.

BOY, YOU RACED THOUGHT AND ALMOST WON.

AND YOU, LORD LOKI, WERE DEFEATED NOT BY A GIANT EITHER, BUT BY A WILDFIRE.

YOU DID ADMIRABLY.

43

AND YOU, THOR, DRANK NOT FROM A HORN BUT FROM THE OCEAN.

YOU DRANK MORE THAN ANYONE EVER BEFORE, SO THAT WE NOW SEE ISLANDS THAT WERE ONCE COVERED.

THE CAT WASN'T A CAT, BUT WAS THE MIDGARD SERPENT ENTWINED AROUND THE WORLD.

YOU CAME DANGEROUSLY CLOSE TO FORCING IT TO LET GO OF ITS TAIL, WHICH WOULD HAVE WRECKED THE WORLD.

AS FOR THE LAST CHALLENGE, THAT WAS NO CRONE, BUT TIME, WHOM NO ONE CAN EVER BEAT.

ANYTHING ANYONE TRIES WILL FAIL, BUT YOU, THOR, CAME CLOSER TO BEATING IT THAN ANYONE.

I WILL DESTROY YOU FOR TRICKING ME!

WE KNEW YOU WOULD ACT THIS WAY, AND THAT IS WHY WE USED OUR MAGIC TO BEAT YOUR STRENGTH.

HAVING BEATEN YOU, WE NOW ASK THAT YOU—

NEVER LOOK FOR US AGAIN!

REMEMBER HOW YOU TOLD ME THAT STRENGTH WOULD ALWAYS BEAT THINKING?

YES, SO?

WELL, THE GIANTS KNEW YOUR STRENGTH COULD BEAT THEM SO THEY PLAYED A TRICK. A TRICK SO GOOD, THEY TRICKED *ME*, THE TRICKSTER.

THEY OUT-THOUGHT YOU, AND THEY DIDN'T BEAT MY STRENGTH!

SO YOU WERE WRONG.

YES, REALLY.

NO, NOT REALLY.

NO, *NOT* REALLY.

YES.

NO.

OH, BROTHER, NOT AGAIN ...

GLOSSARY

ASGARD: the home of the Norse gods

CRONE: an old woman

LEMMINGS: small, short-tailed, furry-footed rodents that live in northern regions

LOKI: the trickster in Norse mythology, often identified as Thor's brother

MIDGARD SERPENT: a giant serpent that circles the earth, according to Norse legend

MJOLNIR: Thor's magic hammer

MORTAL: a being that dies

ODIN: father of the Norse gods

THOR: the Norse god of Thunder

UTGARD–LOKI: king of the Norse giants

pencil from page 32